YOUR KNOWLEDGE HAS VALUE

Bibliographic information published by the German National Library:

The German National Library lists this publication in the National Bibliography;
detailed bibliographic data are available on the Internet at http://dnb.dnb.de .

Imprint:

Copyright © 2014 GRIN Verlag, Open Publishing GmbH
Print and binding: Books on Demand GmbH, Norderstedt Germany
ISBN: 978-3-668-20546-8

This book at GRIN:

http://www.grin.com/en/e-book/321156/a-short-introduction-to-west-indian-litera-
ture-mary-seacole-as-an-example

Friederike Börner

A short introduction to West Indian Literature. Mary Seacole as an example for Jamaican Female Writers

GRIN Publishing

GRIN - Your knowledge has value

Since its foundation in 1998, GRIN has specialized in publishing academic texts by students, college teachers and other academics as e-book and printed book. The website www.grin.com is an ideal platform for presenting term papers, final papers, scientific essays, dissertations and specialist books.

Visit us on the internet:

http://www.grin.com/

http://www.facebook.com/grincom

http://www.twitter.com/grin_com

University of Potsdam

English Department

SoSe 2014

3 LP

Aufbaumodul Literatur- und

Kulturwissenschaft Postkoloniale Literatur &

Kultur (A5LK)

Friederike Börner

Anglistik/Germanistik

Hausarbeit

„A short introduction to West Indian Literature - Mary Seacole as an example for Jamaican Female Writers"

date of submission: 28 July 2014

.

Outline

. Short Introdcution to the West Indian Literature and Overview

The West Indies share the common experience of colonisation, displacement, slavery, emancipation and nationalism - this particular West Indian experience is part of the West Indian culture and of their arts[1]. Even though slavery was abolished between 100 and 50 years ago, it lives on in the memories of the inhabitants of the Caribbean islands. The experience of slavery lead to cynicism and despair as well as to hope and positive thoughts which inspire the West Indian dream of individual freedom and collective independence. Those dreams are shared in the literature of the West Indies.

A development of literature on the Caribbean islands first started in the 18th and 19th century. An explosion of it followed in the 1930s and the late 50s. Topics at this time were an anti-colonial perspective and a search for new definitions and values. However the West Indian literature grew into new dimensions in the late 20th century[2]. Caribbean writers dealt with historical, social and political adjustments on their islands, which were part of their own problems with identity and aesthetics. West Indian literature shows its variety in poetry, prose, fiction and drama. The poetry of the early 70ths was motivated by the Black Power movement and therefore radical and revolutionary. Back then and still nowadays the greatest influence of West Indian literature is the complementary relationship of oral and written traditions of the Caribbean inhabitants[3].

In this work I want to provide a brief overview of the literature development in the West Indies, especially in Jamaica. Therefore I will discuss the language and literature situation in Jamaica and talk about the author Mary Seacole as an example for a female Jamaican writer. A part of my work will be that I discuss the role of women and female characters in Jamaican literature. That is why I decided for Mary Seacole's book

[1] cf. Dabydeen, David & Wilson-Tagoe, Nana. *A Reader's Guide to the Westindian and Black British Literature.* Hatfield: The Bracken Press, 1997. Print p. 13

[2] cf. Dabydeen, David & Wilson-Tagoe, Nana. *A Reader's Guide to the Westindian and Black British Literature.* Hatfield: The Bracken Press, 1997. Print p. 13

[3] Dabydeen, David & Wilson-Tagoe, Nana. *A Reader's Guide to the Westindian and Black British Literature.* Hatfield: The Bracken Press, 1997. Print p. 21

"Wonderful Adventures of Mrs Seacole in Many Lands". At the end of this paper I want t
give an outlook of Jamaican literature and the situation of black literature in the Caribbean.

2. Brief history of Jamaican literature

Discovered by Christopher Columbus in 1494 Jamaica is now
the biggest English-speaking country in the Caribbean. It was occupied by the Spaniards i
1509 and the import of West African Negro slaves started with the arrival of the Spanish
settlers. Therefore Spanish became the first European language spoken in Jamaica. In 1655
England captured the island and continued the import of West African slaves. By 1690
eighty two percent of the population in Jamaica were African slaves[4]. The influence of
African languages on the developing languages was tremendous[5]. English-based pidgi
languages developed together with the influence of Modern English and the African tribal
languages. In the 18th century Jamaican Creole English finally developed from the existing
pidgin languages. In the 19th century the slave trade stopped and brought an end to the
African language influences. Eventually pidgin speakers started to decrease and Jamaica
became creolised.

Jamaica became independent in 1962, until this time the British colony had English
language influences. Nowadays we have two major languages in Jamaica: the Standar
Jamaican English, which is the official language of the country and the Jamaican Creole
English, often referred to as *Jamaican Patwois*. Both languages still influence each other
as they coexist on the island and are in contact everyday. Understanding the language history
of Jamaica is crucial to understand the history of literature on the Caribbean island.

---

[4] Cassidy, F. G. (1971). *The Pidgin Element in Jamaican Creole.* in Hymes, D. H. (eds.), *Pidginization and
creolization of languages; proceedings of a conference held at the University of the West Indies, Mona, Jamaica,
April, 1968.* (pp. 203-221). Cambridge [Eng.: University Press. p. 205

[5] Viereck, Wolfgang, and Karin Viereck. *dtv-Atlas englische Sprache.* München: Deutscher Taschenbuch Verlag
GmbH & Co.KG, 2002. Print. p- 19

Nowadays and back then Jamaican writers struggle with the choice of writing in Jamaican Patwois or Standard English. Standard English is universally better understood and accepted, however Patwois is an important part of Jamaican culture and so distinctly Jamaican, that it cannot be ignored. Famous authors like Joan Andrea Hutchinson or Louise Simone Bennett-Coverly ("Miss Lou") were using Jamaican Patwois and standard English in their writing, showing the high value of Jamaican Patwois sayings and phrases and to express a unique Jamaican essence. Inspite of Patwois being understood and used by most of the Jamaicans it is not the official written language in the country. Therefore poetry and prose written in Patwois always differs in orthography. Although many Jamaican people pledge for an official acceptance of Patwois as a language of education in school, Standard Jamaican English has still the higher prestige in the country. It is only recently due to the popularity of Reggae music, that Patwois gained recognition also in countries outside the Caribbean.

Jamaican art and culture is a mixture of many ethnicities that came to the island over the last centuries. Besides the different European settlers coming to the island and the slave trade forced by the British government, Jamaica also had Chinese and Indian immigrants, who came as indentured workers. Therefore Jamaica has not only a multilingual situation, but also shows its diversity in arts and culture.

. Women & Female Characters in West Indian Literature

Historically the West Indian women were the repositories of oral tradition and folk wisdom in their community. However they only have recently been able to project themselves in written literature. Usually the images of them appearing earlier in the West Indian literature were created by men. But the women of the Caribbean had a central role in history and in their communities of the islands.

For the European settlers women were central for the continuation of the slave system, since they had the ability to produce the labor force. The reality was, that slave women were workers and mothers in an almost spiritual sense[6]. The bond between mother and child was sacred and slave women did everything to protect their children from the planter's utilitarian and commercial view. George Campbell portrayed the Caribbean women in his 1940 poetry as "history makers" or "women stonebreakers"[7]. This image of strong spiritual women changed into various other images due to historical and social changes in the Caribbean region. Some writers created the image of a rural woman, which was usually poor, hardy and abandoned mother with an optimistic view and lovingly committed to her child and her own community. Those rural women possessed a strength and meaning deriving from their sense of shared confidences between her and the people around her. Also the community of the women played a crucial role here[8].

Another image of women in the West Indian literature is the image of an aggressively ambitious urban prostitute or the image of a rural woman in the urban areas trying to survive and earn a living. This new image came up by a disintegration of Caribbean people and separations brought by migration and urban settlements. However the degraded women of the slums often possessed a generosity of spirit despite all their poverty and desperation[9]. Inspite of the bad experiences with slavery and the suffering caused by the oppressors, very few West Indian women have specifically explored social or psychological problems. Caribbean women usually commented on their life and their general social situation.

In the 1940s the Jamaican poet Louise Simone Bennett-Coverley commented on women's view of marriage, racial attitudes or the strength and vulnerability of the Jamaican society. However she saw herself as social commentator and oral performer - her commentary was presented through consciousness of the rural women in Jamaica. Just

---

[6] cf. Dabydeen, David & Wilson-Tagoe, Nana. *A Reader's Guide to the Westindian and Black British Literature.* Hatfield: The Bracken Press, 1997. Print p. 43

[7] Dabydeen, David & Wilson-Tagoe, Nana. *A Reader's Guide to the Westindian and Black British Literature.* Hatfield: The Bracken Press, 1997. Print p. 43

[8] Dabydeen, David & Wilson-Tagoe, Nana. *A Reader's Guide to the Westindian and Black British Literature.* Hatfield: The Bracken Press, 1997. Print p. 43

[9] Dabydeen, David & Wilson-Tagoe, Nana. *A Reader's Guide to the Westindian and Black British Literature.* Hatfield: The Bracken Press, 1997. Print p. 44

recently West Indian writers emerged a consciousness of the Caribbean women. Writers like Merle Hodge, Grace Nichols or Jean Rhys faced topics like cultural confusion about identity, color, prettiness and self-worth of the Caribbean women in their novels. They also dealt with the alienation of the white creole ("half") women from her West Indian background. Another topic in the recent West Indian literature is the evolution of women from a slave to a free person struggling with fear, weaknesses but also triumph. Women in Caribbean literature also search for their own personality and individuality. The consciousness of the role of West Indian women is on the rise, but still needs to be established in the Caribbean literature. In Jamaica, just like on the other Caribbean islands not many women write for their living[10]. This could be the main cause for a paucity of writers. Compared to Black British- or Black American writers, in the Caribbean we find an absence of a tradition of writing women.

4. An example for Jamaican female writers -
Mary Seacole's "Wonderful Adventures of Mrs Seacole in Many Lands"

Mary Seacole was a historical person, a pioneering nurse and a heroine of the Crimean war, who overcame double prejudice due to her Jamaican heritage and being a Victorian self-made woman. She was born as Mary Jane Grant in Kingston, Jamaica in 1805, twentynine years before slavery was abolished. Her father was a Scottish soldier and her mother was Jamaican. In her childhood Mary learned nursing skills from her mother, who kept a boarding house for invalid soldiers in Kingston. In 1836 she married Edwin Seacole but the marriage was short-lived due to Edwin Seacole's death in 1844. Mary Seacole was a frequent traveller, she visited Cuba, Haiti and the Bahamas as well as Central America and Britain. On her trips she complemented her skills in traditional medicine mixed with European medical ideas which made her a skilled and well-known nurse. She went to Panama to treat tropical diseases like cholera and yellow fever and was able to save

---

[10] Dabydeen, David & Wilson-Tagoe, Nana. *A Reader's Guide to the Westindian and Black British Literature.* Hatfield: The Bracken Press, 1997. Print p. 45

many lives. In 1854 she went to Britain to apply as an army nurse in the Crimean war. She got refused and decided to go anyway by herself. She founded the trip and established the "British Hotel" near Balaclava to provide a shelter and nursing home for sick and wounded officers. She also visited the battlefield during the war to nurse the wounded soldiers. Due to her heroic actions she became known as "Mother Seacole". After the war she returned to England, where she became well-known and honored. In 1857 a benefit festival was held in the Royal Surrey Garden. In the same year she published her autobiography, which became an instant success and was reprinted the same year. She died on the 14 May 1881. Although she became totally forgotten by the 20th century British public, Mary Seacole remains one of the most significant woman of her times. She was extraordinary in terms of her fame and the respect she commanded from the British nobility[11].

In her autobiography Mary Seacole graduates from her celebrity status in Jamaica as a "creole doctress" to a legendary status in the Crimea and in Britain as "Mother Seacole" - guardian and purveyor of English values away from home[12]. Her narrative of adventures and travel depict her as a rootless and restless wandering West Indian woman, which is actually a distinctive feature of post colonial and colonial literature. The main topic in her narrative is the Crimean war, depicted as a patriotic and heroic event. Mary Seacole's view on war is full of glorification, being supportive on the wounded soldiers. "What a delight should I not experience if I could be useful to my own 'sons', suffering for a cause it was so glorious to fight and bleed for![13]" In another passage Mary Seacole describes an officer servant "lying crouched in a rifle pit, having "pots" at the Russians, or keeping watch along line of trenches, or, stripped to his shirt shovelling powder and shot into the great guns, whose

---

[11] Dabydeen, David & Wilson-Tagoe, Nana. *A Reader's Guide to the Westindian and Black British Literature.* Hatfield: The Bracken Press, 1997. Print p. 135

[12] Paquet, Sandra Pouchet. "The Enigma of arrival: 'The Wonderful Adventures of Mrs. Seacole in Many Lands.'" *African American Review.* (Dec 22, 1992): 1-11. The Free Library. http://www.thefreelibrary.com/_/print/PrintArticle.aspx?id=13893635. 26.07.2014. p. 1/11

[13] Dabydeen, David & Wilson-Tagoe, Nana. *A Reader's Guide to the Westindian and Black British Literature.* Hatfield: The Bracken Press, 1997. Print p. 136

steady roar broke the evening calm"[14]. The alliterations and the rhythm of the passage cause patriotic emotions of the Victorian readership of her book. Mary Seacole's romantic patriotism is described in many different parts of the book in a poetic language. She shows a devotion to the Queen and the Empire, at the funeral of a high officer she proudly and sadly touches the Union Jack. All this behavior is contrary to the racism she experienced by the British people towards black people, the plundering and the partitioning of Africa by the Europeans and the colonial repression in Jamaica which had only just emerged from slavery. In her religious fervour, her moral outlook and her militaristic patriotism as a Victorian figure, Mary Seacole appears to be a ludicrous figure because of her color and her own mixed ancestry. During her stay in Britain she also received racial insults on account of her skin color and as a result of defending black people and showing pride in African achievements[15]. She states, that she is proud of the fact, that many free Africans in Latin America have become magistrates, government officials, civic leaders and other high positions. Contrary to that she is proud to be a part of the British Empire and proud to be half-white. Referring to herself as "yellow woman" or "brown woman" she also states at the beginnging of her book, that her good character traits come from her white father:

"I am a Creole, and have good Scotch blood coursing through my veins. Many people have traced to my Scottish blood that energy and activity which are not always found in the Creole race, and which have carried me to so many varied scenes: and perhaps they are right."[16]

Not only being proud on her white ancestry, Mary Seacole also shows a vicious contempt for black people and all non-British nationalities in her narrative. Moreover she is giving stereotypical descriptions of Maltese, Greek and Turkish people, which would have appealed to the xenophobian Victorian reading public. Her patriotism and her attitude towards non-British people reveal her split personality. On the one hand Mary Seacole is

---

[14] Dabydeen, David & Wilson-Tagoe, Nana. *A Reader's Guide to the Westindian and Black British Literature.* Hatfield: The Bracken Press, 1997. Print p. 136
[15] Dabydeen, David & Wilson-Tagoe, Nana. *A Reader's Guide to the Westindian and Black British Literature.* Hatfield: The Bracken Press, 1997. Print p. 137
[16] Dabydeen, David & Wilson-Tagoe, Nana. *A Reader's Guide to the Westindian and Black British Literature.* Hatfield: The Bracken Press, 1997. Print p. 138

sensitive to her black ancestry and aware of the racism against black people. But on the other hand she shows her contempt for black people, non-British and she is happy to declare her half-whiteness. Therefore her narrative yields an unique insight to divided loyalties of colonial people due to their mixed blood and heritages and the "loss of their home"[17].

Another aspect of Mary Seacole's narrative is the womanhood in Victorian England and her achievements as a free self-made female. Again we find a contradiction in Mary Seacole's personality. On the one hand she is committed to the English values of her time, on the other hand she stands for a radical brand of feminism. After the death of her husband she decides to remain as a widow and therefore an "unprotected female"[18]. She is describing herself always in action and in a battle with the world. She is also not afraid to compete with a man and she knows about her value (eg. "the work of half a dozen men"[19]). Her personality and her efforts contrast with a man-dominated housebound Victorian woman. However, she still embraces certain conventions of Victorian womanhood, when writing about herself or comparing herself with other women at this time. She makes fun of "those French lady writers who desire to enjoy the privileges of man, with the irresponsibility of the other sex [20]" or complains about women in New Grenada who dress in trousers and walk on the street "in unfeminine fashion[21]".

Mary Seacole is a rebellious, independent and competitive Jamaican woman, who is taking action to creolize and feminize the European male space. But her achievements are presented as individual accomplishments, she is celebrating her own devotion to the Empire

---

[17] Dabydeen, David & Wilson-Tagoe, Nana. *A Reader's Guide to the Westindian and Black British Literature.* Hatfield: The Bracken Press, 1997. Print p. 138
[18] Paquet, Sandra Pouchet. "The Enigma of arrival: 'The Wonderful Adventures of Mrs. Seacole in Many Lands.'" *African American Review.* (Dec 22, 1992): 1-11. The Free Library. http://www.thefreelibrary.com/_/print/PrintArticle.aspx?id=13893635. 26.07.2014. p. 3/11
[19] Paquet, Sandra Pouchet. "The Enigma of arrival: 'The Wonderful Adventures of Mrs. Seacole in Many Lands.'" *African American Review.* (Dec 22, 1992): 1062-4783. The Free Library. http://www.thefreelibrary.com/_/print/PrintArticle.aspx?id=13893635. 26.07.2014. p. 3/11
[20] Paquet, Sandra Pouchet. "The Enigma of arrival: 'The Wonderful Adventures of Mrs. Seacole in Many Lands.'" *African American Review.* (Dec 22, 1992): 1062-4783. The Free Library. http://www.thefreelibrary.com/_/print/PrintArticle.aspx?id=13893635. 26.07.2014. p. 3/11
[21] Paquet, Sandra Pouchet. "The Enigma of arrival: 'The Wonderful Adventures of Mrs. Seacole in Many Lands.'" *African American Review.* (Dec 22, 1992): 1062-4783. The Free Library. http://www.thefreelibrary.com/_/print/PrintArticle.aspx?id=13893635. 26.07.2014. p. 3/11

and her freedom as embodied in the British military. Especially during her time in the Crimea we cannot find any suggestion, that her intention was to change the status of a Black West Indian woman in general. However her narrative is also a success story. She is perceived heroic by the British empire and she achieves the authority and recognition to publish her autobiography. It is the success story of a creole woman, becoming famous and well-known due to her extraordinary skills and her ambition. She is adopting to the values of her time, but still is rebellious enough to fight for her own achievements and to become the person, she wants to be. She is celebrated as a woman of color in a community of white men during the Crimean war and she is a rootless traveler without a home, but also without needing a home. The Crimean war is a public and political event, that gives her life meaning, it is not a West Indian phenomenon, giving her the chance to live in a new community[22]. Her narrative reflects the post colonial psychology of restlessness and rootlessness and the fight for an individual freedom and appreciation by her former oppressors.

5. Conclusion and Outlook

Seacole represents a different form of post colonial literature in her writing. She is not talking about homecoming or a return to her African roots, but she is adapting to a New World identity. Mary Seacole sees the British Empire has part of her identity as well as her mixed background and her pride in being a creole woman. She is exploring the freedom through her sheer will and energy and she forces a redefinition of her creole Jamaican self from a colonial, marginalized woman. She becomes a heroine and a keeper of English values in the British Empire.

We still can see her contradictions in her narrative, probably a typical aspect of all post colonial literature dealing with identity and finding a place in the new world. However,

---

[22] Paquet, Sandra Pouchet. "The Enigma of arrival: 'The Wonderful Adventures of Mrs. Seacole in Many Lands.'" *African American Review*. (Dec 22, 1992): 1062-4783. The Free Library. http://www.thefreelibrary.com/_/print/PrintArticle.aspx?id=13893635. 26.07.2014. p. 4-5/11

she is a symbol for a strong and independent Caribbean woman, who achieved appreciation outside the West Indian islands. She is one of the women, George Campbell would call "history makers"[23] presenting an image of the spiritual, optimistic and strong woman who is lovingly committed to her community or her ideals. Mary Seacole made the first step to establish a British-West Indian literature and to show the independence of former slaves struggling to find their individual freedom.

---

[23] Dabydeen, David & Wilson-Tagoe, Nana. *A Reader's Guide to the Westindian and Black British Literature*. Hatfield: The Bracken Press, 1997. Print p. 43

6. References
6. 1 Books

Alexander, Ziggi and Dewjee, Audrey. "Editors' Introduction." *The Wonderful Adventures of Mrs. Seacole in Many Lands*. By Mary Seacole. Bristol: Falling Wall. Bachelard, Gaston, 1984. Print.

Bailey, B. L. *Jamaican Creole syntax: a transformational approach*. Cambridge: Cambridge U.P. , 1966. Print.

Brathwaite, E. K. *The development of Creole society in Jamaica 1770-1820*. Oxford: Clarendon Press, 1971. Print.

Cassidy, F. G. *The Pidgin Element in Jamaican Creole*. in Hymes, D. H. (eds.), *Pidginization and creolization of languages; proceedings of a conference held at the University of the West Indies, Mona, Jamaica, April, 1968*. (pp. 203-221). Cambridge [Eng.: University Press, 1971. Print.

Chamberlin, Edward J. *Come back to me my language. Poetry and the West Indies*. Illinois: University of Illinois Press, 1993. Print.

Cooper, C. *Sound clash: Jamaican dancehall culture at large*. New York: Palgrave Macmillan, 2004. Print.

Dabydeen, David & Wilson-Tagoe, Nana. *A Reader's Guide to the Westindian and Black British Literature*. Hatfield: The Bracken Press, 1997. Print

Devonish, H. Dancehall Transnation - Language, Lit/Orature, and Global Jamaica. *Sound clash: Jamaican dancehall culture at large* (pp. 279-301). New York: Palgrave Macmillan, 2004. Print.

Hinrichs, L. *Codeswitching on the web English and Jamaican Creole in e-mail communication.* Amsterdam: J. Benjamins Pub, 2006. Print.

Hymes, D. H. *Pidginization and creolization of languages; proceedings of a conference held at the University of the West Indies, Mona, Jamaica, April, 1968..* Cambridge [Eng.: University Press, 1971. Print.

Lalla, Barbara. *Defining Jamaican Fiction. Marronage and the Discourse of Survival.* Alabama: University Alabama Press, 1996. Print.

Viereck, Wolfgang, and Karin Viereck. *dtv-Atlas englische Sprache.* München: Deutscher Taschenbuch Verlag GmbH & Co.KG, 2002. Print.

6. 2 Websites

Victory for Jamaican patois! - Columns - Jamaica Observer Mobile. (n.d.). *Jamaica Observer: Jamaican News Online – the Best of Jamaican Newspapers - JamaicaObserver.com.* Retrieved February 16, 2013, from http://m.jamaicaobserver.com/mobile/columns/Victory-for-Jamaican-patois-_13564541

The story of Jamaican Literature - *Visual and Performing Arts Jamaica*.
http://www.vpaj.org/. Retrieved July 22, 2014 from
http://www.vpaj.org/arts-in-ja/jamaican-literature

Paquet, Sandra Pouchet. "The Enigma of arrival: 'The Wonderful Adventures of Mrs.
Seacole in Many Lands.'" *African American Review*. (Dec 22, 1992): 1-11. The Free
Library.   http://www.thefreelibrary.com/_/print/PrintArticle.aspx?id=13893635.
26.07.2014.

YOUR KNOWLEDGE HAS VALUE

- We will publish your bachelor's and
  master's thesis, essays and papers

- Your own eBook and book -
  sold worldwide in all relevant shops

- Earn money with each sale

Upload your text at www.GRIN.com
and publish for free